Marisol's Mystery

Leslie Arnott
Illustrated by Sergi Camara

Rigby
A Harcourt Achieve Imprint

www.Rigby.com
1-800-531-5015

It was six days before Marisol's birthday party.
She was playing with her cat, Fluffy.
Suddenly she looked around and Fluffy was gone!

Marisol saw a tail by the door.
When she looked inside, she found
Fluffy and a big brown box.

Marisol pulled, but she couldn't move the box!

"The note says this box is for someone special," Marisol told Fluffy.

"Who could that be?" she asked.

"And what could be inside?

This is a mystery!"

The next night, Papá came home
with a yellow helmet.

"Why do you need a helmet?"
Marisol asked him.

"It's not for me," said Papá.
"It's for someone special."

The next morning, Mamá brought home a small bell.

"Why do you need a bell?"
Marisol asked.

"It's not for me," said Mamá.
"It's for someone special."

The next day, Marisol's sister came home with a pump behind her back.

"Anita, why do you need a pump?"
Marisol asked.

"It's not for me," said Anita.
"It's for someone special."

Later Marisol went to look
at the box again.
She thought about everything
she had seen.
Then she put ideas together
to solve the mystery.

"I think I've got it!" she said.

At last it was Marisol's birthday.
Papá and Mamá brought out
the big box.
What a sight it was!

"It's a bike, isn't it?" asked Marisol.
"Am I right?"

"You were close!" said Mamá
and Papá.

"Thanks!" said Marisol.
"I like my scooter even better
than a bike!"